JUDAH SMITH

BESTSELLING AUTHOR OF *JESUS IS* _____ .
LEAD PASTOR OF THE CITY CHURCH, SEATTLE, WASHINGTON

LOVELIKEJESUS

REACHING OTHERS WITH PASSION AND PURPOSE

Regal

For more information and
special offers from Regal Books, email us at
subscribe@regalbooks.com

Published by Regal
From Gospel Light
Ventura, California, U.S.A.
www.regalbooks.com
Printed in the U.S.A.

ISBN 978-0-8307-6641-3 (trade paper)

Rights for publishing this book outside the U.S.A. or in non-English
languages are administered by Gospel Light Worldwide, an international
not-for-profit ministry. For additional information, please visit
www.glww.org, email info@glww.org, or write to Gospel Light Worldwide,
1957 Eastman Avenue, Ventura, CA 93003, U.S.A.

To order copies of this book and other Regal products in
bulk quantities, please contact us at 1-800-446-7735.

CONTENTS

FOREWORD

Our Lord's greatest commandment was and is to go out and make disciples of all the nations (see Matthew 28:19). In today's terms, we would call that "soul winning." This book is an excellent resource for everyone—from new believers to veteran Christians—who wants to draw closer to the Father in a practical manner. It is one thing to read the Word of God, but it is something entirely different to actually walk it out, to go out and meet the needs of the people around us.

The greatest sermons are not preached from behind a pulpit but rather from the way we live our lives. The world even knows this truth, which is perfectly illustrated in the simple phrase "Actions speak louder than words." We may not all be called into full-time ministry, but we all are called to minister to those around us at all times. Judah Smith has written an excellent book that will inspire you to get out of your seat and into the streets.

Matthew Barnett
Senior Pastor
LA Dream Center

PREFACE

Recently I found myself leading an impromptu Bible study with some very un-churched people. They were all in their twenties, so at thirty-four years old I was the old guy. That didn't feel very good, but apparently my years of experience convinced them I had everything figured out about life, marriage, God and happiness. So I ran with that. I figured in that setting, I needed all the help I could get.

Part of me wishes I could say I delivered a flawless theological discourse that proved beyond a doubt the basic tenets of the Christian faith. But I'm not that smart. So instead, I spoke on John 3:16 and simply told them about Jesus.

I told them who Jesus is, why He came to earth and died, and what that meant for our day-to-day life. I told them that God is a good God and that He's not mad at us. I said that life can be tough and sometimes we do things we shouldn't do, but Jesus is on our side and never gives up on us. I preached hope.

It was pretty much the most basic explanation of the gospel ever given. But they had never heard it before, and to them it was earth shattering. After I finished, person after person told me how much my words meant to them.

Judah Smith

It was an eye-opener for me. I watched as the same gospel and the same Jesus that have been preached for two thousand years continued to compel lost people to turn to Jesus. Logic and debates and threats of judgment could not have accomplished in a year what the good news of Jesus' love did in a few short minutes.

I think sometimes we take the gospel for granted. We've heard it and experienced it and even preached about it so much that it doesn't seem that amazing anymore. But then we spend time with real people with real problems, and we are brought back to this simple truth: Jesus is enough.

The longer I pastor people, the more convinced I am that there is nothing like the love of Jesus. That is the bottom line when it comes to evangelism. The focus of our conversation and our preaching is not hell or sin or self-effort. It's Jesus.

I first wrote the book you are holding when I was the youth pastor at The City Church over ten years ago. It was titled *Soulseekers* at the time, and true to my context many of the illustrations and comments are directed at young people or youth pastors.

Now I'm the lead pastor at the same church. I face different challenges and greater responsibilities, but the truths and principles described here have not changed. If anything, my conviction that Jesus is the answer to the needs of humanity has only increased. This conviction is reflected in the new book title: *Love Like Jesus*. I have made a few updates for the sake of flow and consistency, but the bulk of the book has remained unchanged from what I wrote ten years ago.

I can think of no greater joy and privilege than introducing people to grace. Thank you for sharing that passion.

Judah Smith, 2013

9

INTRODUCTION

It is my desire that as you read this book your heart would be captured with a consuming passion for people. In these days where many see human life as less than significant, it is my aim that you find in your heart a new resolve to discover the significance of each human life. In preparing the messages and writings that make up this book, I came across a quote that sums up the life work of William Booth. It also encapsulates the message of this book:

> For over thirty years the Salvation Army and William Booth in particular were subject to some of the most vile persecutions Christians suffered in modern times. But the General lived to see the day his army would be honored around the world. His own King Edward VII invited him to Buckingham Palace in 1904. All the persecution and trials of the previous decades must have seemed insignificant to Booth as he heard King Edward say, "You are doing a good work—a great work, General Booth."
>
> When the King asked Booth to write in his autograph album, the old man—now

seventy-five—bent forward, took the pen, and summed up his life's work:

Your Majesty,
Some men's ambition is art,
Some men's ambition is fame,
Some men's ambition is gold,
My ambition is the souls of men.[1]

What you are about to read is not an exhaustive resource or a theological discourse. It is simply the study of a passage of Scripture that is changing my life. In the last few months, it has become the theme of our youth ministry, Generation Church, and I believe it can raise the water level of soul winning in your youth church or place of influence as it has in ours. May our ambition become the souls of men!

Note
1. Paul Lee Tan, *Encyclopedia of 7,700 Illustrations* (Rockville, MD: Assurance Publishers, 1979).

LOVE LIKE JESUS

1

THE CHALLENGE OF **COMPASSION** FOR PEOPLE

HAVE YOU EVER BEFRIENDED SOMEONE OR GONE OUT OF YOUR WAY TO HELP SOMEBODY WHO YOU KNEW IN THE BACK OF YOUR MIND WOULD PAY YOU BACK? Have you ever found yourself befriending an acquaintance only because of the money he or she had or the connections he or she possessed?

Our motives for loving people must rise higher than this. Luke 6:32-33 says, "But if you love those who love you, what credit is that to you? For even sinners love those who love them. And if you do good to those who do good to you, what credit is that to you? For even sinners do the same."

Motivation is everything! Well, maybe not everything, but close. This is where reaching people for Christ starts. Before we go any further, ask yourself, *Why do I want to reach people?* Your response to that question means everything.

Our culture tells us to set goals and reach them, but it never asks why. In God's kingdom, He requires the "why" to be answered. A. W. Tozer remarks:

> The Test by which all conduct must finally be judged is motive. As water cannot rise higher than its source, so the moral quality in an act can never be higher than the motive that inspires it.[1]

Ultimately, our motivation for saving and restoring human lives affects our level of lasting influence. Jesus was motivated by a true and genuine love for each individual; therefore, His ability to reach people and leave lasting change was extraordinary.

We should allow God to investigate the motivation of our heart. Do we see past the sin and love the sinner? Do we truly value the person regardless of whether they love us back? Will we continue to love them even if they never change? Let's take a moment and whisper a prayer asking God to purify the motives of our hearts.

JESUS IS THE ULTIMATE EXAMPLE

Jesus is our ultimate example of living the "call to people." Throughout Christ's ministry on earth, there is one simple phrase that could sum up His heart toward people: He was moved with compassion. Using Jesus as my example, I have prayed many times that I would love people more, give my life for others and be moved with compassion. But what does that look like? Did I even know what I was praying for?

Before we get into the heart of this book, we need to answer the challenge of compassion for people. First, we need to understand what compassion is. Second, we must determine how to get it. Without compassion, our efforts to reach people will start out strong on an emotional high and then slowly fade as our lives get busy and we realize the immense cost of getting involved in people's lives.

JESUS IS COMPASSIONATE

In the Gospel of Mark, chapter 1, we find a story in which Jesus demonstrates true compassion for us. Jesus was walking and talking with His disciples when a man afflicted with leprosy fell to his knees in front of Jesus and begged, "If You are willing, You can make me clean" (verse 40).

Mark records Jesus' response in verses 41-42: "Then Jesus, moved with compassion, stretched out

His hand and touched him, and said to him, 'I am willing; be cleansed.' As soon as He had spoken, immediately the leprosy left him, and he was cleansed."

I believe Jesus used this opportunity to instruct both His disciples and us by demonstrating how we should respond to the challenge of exercising compassion for people.

As we look at this story, we must recognize what lepers represented to society in Jesus' day. Leprosy and the infections that it caused literally rotted away the flesh of their bodies to the point of death. I believe that this is a picture of modern-day sinners. Sin is a disease that slowly rots the life out of people to the point of death.

A young lady in our youth ministry recently e-mailed me her testimony. Her story illustrates the terrible effect of sin. Like leprosy, sin was eating away her life, but Jesus wasn't afraid to stretch out His hand and rescue her:

> Almost two years ago, I lost my virginity when I was raped. I proceeded to get into many bad physical relationships, started drinking and struggled with an eating disorder. There were countless nights I would sit in my room, weeping and begging God

to either deliver me or kill me. I hated who I was becoming, but I didn't know how to get out of it. I struggled for a long time, and my behavior ended up getting me kicked out of my home. I remember the day well. I had gone to the doctor who diagnosed me with three sexually transmitted diseases; one of them was incurable.

That night after work, I got in my car. I had a big bottle of vodka and my plan was to get drunk and kill myself. I thought that nobody would ever want to love me. I was completely alone and miserable, and living out of my car. I began to weep and all I could say was "Jesus" over and over again. As soon as I began to say His name, I heard a voice say, "Go to church." It was a Wednesday night around 8:45 and I knew Generation Church was probably almost over. So I made God a deal. I told Him that I would go, but if He didn't meet me that night, I was going to take my life.

I went into the sanctuary and sat about six rows back. People were at the altar worshiping and praying, and I just sat and cried. Pastor Judah must have seen me and he came over and put his hand on my head to pray for me. I was kind of afraid because I thought maybe God was

19

telling him everything that I had done, and I didn't want all my dirt exposed. I was embarrassed. Yet I felt the Spirit of God so heavily that I began to sob! After a while, he walked away to go pray for someone else. One of the female leaders came over and asked how I was doing. I lost it and told her everything, even about the liquor in my car and my plans to commit suicide. Literally, the minute I finished talking, Pastor Jude called out over the microphone, "I don't know why, but for some reason I know there is someone here, you are being completely oppressed, you feel there is no way out, and you want to kill yourself. But tonight God wants to set you free. Come forward and God is going to deliver you." The leader walked with me and I went forward.

Let me tell you, something broke in me that night. I was completely set free. I actually wanted to live again. I met my cadre leader [cell-group leader] that night and she prayed for me. Afterward she leaned over, hugged me and told me that she loved me. For the first time, I heard God speak directly to me. He said, "She just met you and she loves you, but I made you. Imagine how much more I love you." That night I broke all my secular CDs, turned over my alcohol to Pastor Judah and gave my life over to Jesus. God topped it off by healing me of my STD at camp a few months later.

Since that night I have never been the same. I have never gone back. Although I still struggle sometimes, I am seeing God's faithfulness in my life like never before. I am so grateful, and I just wanted to say thanks.

As I read this young lady's story, I again am reminded of God's immeasurable compassion and our responsibility to express it to our generation. I am so thankful that Jesus is still in the healing business. The kind of compassion Jesus demonstrates isn't just a feeling of pity for us; He actually moves on our behalf. In both the leper's and the young lady's stories, there are three ingredients of compassion: stretched out, touched, and spoke.

JESUS STRETCHED OUT

As Jesus was moved with compassion for the leper, He "stretched out His hand" (Mark 1:41). A dictionary defines "stretch" as "to reach out or to extend."[2]

In order to possess the same compassion Jesus did, we must be willing to stretch beyond our current comfort zone.

This may mean reaching beyond what is convenient, comfortable or routine. It may mean giving more than token sympathy to people we see in need. We must stretch out. In 1 Peter 1:22, Peter uses the word "fervently" to describe the kind of love we are to have for one another. "Fervently" actually means "to stretch."[3] The message is clear: We must remain fervent about reaching people with the love of Christ.

JESUS TOUCHED

Jesus stretched out His hand to the leper in order to touch him. As Jesus did this, His disciples must have been in absolute shock. Nobody touched lepers—leprosy made a person ceremonially unclean. The leper himself must have pulled back when Jesus unexpectedly touched him. Most likely, it had been a long time since anybody had even been near him. Yet our Jesus wasn't afraid to touch him in order to meet his need.

We must follow our Savior's example and touch the lives of sinners. This may mean listening, meeting practical needs, or simply being a friend to a lonely person at school. Sure, if we touch people we might risk their pulling away from us or not accepting us. However, if we never touch the lives of people, we will never truly know what it is to be moved with compassion. We will never experience the fulfillment of watching a life being transformed.

My perspective began to change when I started reaching out to my classmates in high school. During my junior year, I started to look for new or lonely-looking classmates to eat lunch with.

One day when I walked into the lunchroom, one guy immediately stood out to me. He looked like a prime candidate. I walked over to the long, empty table that he was sitting at and introduced myself, "Hi, I'm Judah. What's your name?"

He looked up in shock. "Uh, I'm Julius." I never did ask him if I could sit down and eat lunch with him; I just did. He looked like an athlete with all the gear on.

"So do you play basketball?" I asked.

He reluctantly responded, "Uh, yeah, you too?"

"Yup!" That was all it took for Julius and me to become close friends. During basketball season, I gave him rides to and from practice. Eventually, he came to church with me and got saved! Sometimes

23

I don't think we realize how simple it is to stretch out and touch someone.

JESUS SPOKE

After Jesus touched the leper, He spoke to the leper. Just think about that: Jesus loved this leper so much that He took the time to speak to him. Jesus also loves the young lady whose testimony we just read. He loves her so much that He spoke to her and told her that He loves her.

In order to convey Jesus' love to others, we must be willing to be the voice of Jesus and speak the Word of God to people. As we do this, we will fully experience the compassion of Jesus flowing through us.

JUST DO COMPASSION

One of my heroes in youth ministry is Pastor Jeanne Mayo. The first time she came to speak at one of our youth conferences, I was amazed as she stopped, hugged and talked to each of the people who waited to talk to her. She met individuals with a genuineness that made them feel special. As I observed her, I thought, *I wish I could love young people like that.*

A few weeks ago, I was listening to one of her CDs and discovered the secret to her genuine compassion for young people. She divulged that in her early days of ministry, she didn't always feel like loving people; but as she simply started meeting people's needs, the feelings came.

Too often we sit around waiting for our emotions to motivate us to go out and reach people. When that doesn't happen, we conclude that God must not be calling us to reach people because we don't feel anything. As a result, we do nothing.

I have a new challenge for you. Just start! As you start stretching, touching and speaking to people, the feelings will come. This is living a life of faith, not a life based on feelings.

Personally, I have been challenged like never before to go out and reach people. What I will share with you in the next several chapters is a simple study of the challenges some of Christ's disciples faced in the process of being called to reach people. Luke 5 describes how Jesus calls His disciples to be fishers of men. In this passage, we see several principles that will change the way we view our Christian influence. As I have been studying this passage and walking out the principles, I can honestly say that my life and love for people have changed. My prayer is that yours will be transformed as well.

A PRAYERFUL PLACE

*Lord, I pray that You will change my
motivations. Give me a pure heart for people.
Teach me about Your compassion and help me
count the cost of reaching people. Move me
beyond pity for others and help me to touch those
whom I wouldn't otherwise care about. Show me
the people who need You most. Help me to stretch
beyond my comfort zone. Change my perspective
and cause me to love people with a sincere heart.
Jesus, move me with Your compassion!*

26

Notes
  1. Harry Verloegh, *The Quotable Tozer I* (Camp Hill, PA: Christian Publica-
     tions, 1984), p. 133.
  2. *Merriam-Webster's Collegiate Dictionary*, 10th ed., s.v. "stretch."
  3. Bible Explorer, *Strong's Concordance* (Austin, TX: Epiphany Software,
     1999), CD-ROM, s.v. "fervently."

2

THE CHALLENGE OF
CONSECRATION
WITHOUT ISOLATION

AS I WAS SITTING COMFORTABLY IN MY BROWN LEATHER DESK CHAIR AND STUDYING MY BIBLE, I THOUGHT ABOUT THE SEVEN-PART PREACHING SERIES THAT I HAD JUST COMPLETED ON THE SUBJECT OF PURITY. I was feeling pretty good about my own success in this area. Sitting there feeling so pure, I began reading in Luke 5 about the disciples washing their nets.

As I finished verse 2, the Holy Spirit said to me in His own direct way, "Have you gone washing and forgotten to go fishing?" In other words, He was asking, "When is the last time you went catching with your nets instead of just washing them over and over?"

Ouch! The Holy Spirit reminded me that just as the purpose of clean nets is to catch fish, so too the purpose of our purity is to reach people.

Don't get me wrong: I don't mean to imply that our success in evangelism depends solely on our purity. In reality, both our right-standing before God and our ability to live in purity come from Jesus, not from our efforts. That means that we can't boast about our purity or look down on others who are less pure; likewise, if we sin we shouldn't give up on ever helping anyone else.

The fact that Jesus helps us conquer sin is good news that we can't keep to ourselves. Our purity, when mixed with love and humility, can be a powerful source of hope for people trapped by sin.

BECOMING FULL-TIME FOLLOWERS

Jesus used this story to teach His disciples about fishing for men. At the time Jesus had this encounter with Peter, James and John, they were just part-time followers of Him. Most theologians agree that this account in Luke 5 is their third call to discipleship. The first call came in John 1 and the second call came in Matthew 4; therefore, we know that Jesus already had been training and talking to them about His passion and mandate for people.

Discipleship finds its greatest expression in reaching and loving people. Here in Luke 5, we see that some of the disciples who loved to hear Jesus teach and to see Him do miracles had not yet given up everything to follow Him full-time. That was about to change.

Jesus was preaching by the lake of Gennesaret. His words were so powerful that the people pressed forward, crowding Him, so He decided to get in a boat and teach from the water. He looked for Peter, who was gone from his boat washing his nets, to ask him to put his boat back in the water and push out a little bit so that He could continue preaching.

After he finished preaching, Jesus asked Peter to launch out into the deep water and catch some fish. Even though Peter had fished all night and caught nothing, he took Jesus at His word and obeyed. As soon as Peter let down his net to catch fish, he caught so many fish that his nets started to break and he had to get help from his partners.

Peter must have realized this was a supernatural catch of fish and that Jesus was more than just a good teacher, because Peter immediately declared himself a sinner and Jesus, Lord. Then Jesus called Peter, James and John to start catching people instead of fish: "Do not be afraid. From now on you will catch men" (Luke 5:10). Needless to say, they responded to Jesus' call, left their fish and boats behind, and followed Jesus full-time.

29

LOSING TOUCH WITH THE SEA

As we can see from the end of the story, the purpose of this story isn't fish—it's people! When Jesus went looking for the fishermen, they were gone washing their nets. Admirably, these men, after working hard all night without success, were preparing their nets to return to sea again. A dirty net eventually would have rotted and fallen apart, which would have made catching fish impossible.

The idea is the same for us. If we are going to catch fish, we need to maintain clean nets. In other words, we need to maintain purity. The problem is that it is easy to get comfortable with our nice, shiny, clean nets and lose touch with the sea.

30

Here's what happens: When we get saved, God pulls us out of a pit of sin and darkness and begins to wash us with His Word. We feel so good that we want to go spend all of our time with other people who have been pulled out of their pits as well. Church becomes "pitless parties" where we sit around and talk about how glad we are that we are no longer in a pit. It is easy to forget that we were pulled out of a pit so that we would help others out of the same desperate situation.

Proverbs 18:1 clearly tells us why we are given to isolation. It states, "A man who isolates himself seeks his own desire." Isolation is centered in self. We find ourselves isolated because we enjoy the comfort it provides us. To go beyond our comfort zone or to make new friends is risky and challenging. Therefore, many people choose the path of least resistance—isolation.

USING OUR NETS
FOR THEIR INTENDED PURPOSE

For most of us, the isolation we are talking about is not sitting at home huddled next to our computer, only catching glimpses of the outside world. However, that spirit can sneak up on us and affect our friendships, attitudes and daily schedules.

31

As a youth pastor, I began to realize that if I didn't make a concerted effort to get out of my office to meet young people and attend some local school sporting events, I would end up isolated. Since that decision, I have changed my schedule. I consistently ask myself this question: Have I gone washing and forgotten to go fishing? Once we realize that our washing has a purpose, we move into a whole new dimension of Christianity!

One of our cadre (small-group) leaders recently discovered how fulfilling life is when we spend it for others. Growing up in the church, she was known as shy, but she now admits it was insecurity. While working with children and youth in the church, she started to overcome her shyness. She realized that with so much to do and so many people to minister to, there was no room for shyness.

That was great, but the Holy Spirit still had more He wanted to do in her life. As she sat in Generation Church and was challenged to reach out to unsaved people, He began to work in her. Up to this point, she loved ministering to Christians, but insecurities held her back from reaching out to unsaved people. Then she experienced a breakthrough.

One afternoon at a park with the children she was watching, she noticed another nanny on a nearby bench. The Holy Spirit clearly spoke to her to step out and talk to this girl. As she obeyed, the Holy Spirit helped her and they talked. Since that conversation, the girl has attended church twice and has absolutely loved it. This Generation Church cadre leader now realizes that she was saved for a purpose—to minister to other people. She has found the joy of using her nets for their intended purpose.

The reason God sets us apart isn't so that we will become isolated. He sets us apart so that we will have strong, healthy nets that are able to pull other

32

people out of the depths of sin. As we continue through Luke 5, we will learn how to be effective in pulling people out.

A PRAYERFUL PLACE

God, forgive me for isolating myself. Continue to purify me so that I will live free from the destructive effects of sin. I am so thankful that You rescued me from the pit of sin. Send me back to rescue those who haven't found the freedom that You have given me. Keep my heart compassionate so that I don't easily forget about others. Don't let my purity be a religious show, but cleanse my life so that I may be a vessel used by You to reach people.

33

3

THE CHALLENGE OF **CARING** ABOUT THE SEEMINGLY INSIGNIFICANT

GROWING UP IN THE CHURCH, I HEARD MANY MES-SAGES AND EXHORTATIONS ON THE SUBJECT OF EVANGELISM. Usually when I heard one of these messages, my first reaction was a sinking feeling in the pit of my stomach. *Oh no*, I thought to myself, *I haven't won my school; I haven't evangelized every person I have met. In fact, it's been awhile since even one of my friends has gotten saved.*

About that time an overwhelming feeling of condemnation and discouragement would try to settle in my heart. So I tried to justify myself: *After all, with the billions of people in the world, what can I do anyway? It's not like I'm Billy Graham, who saw over 1.6 million recorded decisions at his rallies, let alone the hundreds of thousands of other people who heard him preach the gospel.*[1]

IT MATTERS TO THIS ONE

If we start thinking this way, we will be defeated before we start. It is a big world with millions of people who need Jesus Christ. If we don't start with a little, we will never accomplish a lot. We must answer the challenge of caring about the seemingly insignificant. There is no individual who is insignificant to God.

We need the perspective and the passion of the little boy who rescued starfish. Maybe you've heard the story. It goes like this.

A man was walking along the beach one day when he saw thousands of starfish on the shore, washed up by the tide. Then he noticed a young boy throwing starfish back into the sea, one by one. The man approached the young boy, who seemed so determined, and asked, "Young man, do you see that there are thousands of starfish? You can't possibly save them all. What does it matter?"

The little boy paused for a moment, looked at the starfish in his hand and replied with certainty, "Yes, but it matters to this one!"

I am so grateful that my mom recognized the significance of staying home and raising her two children. Although she had plenty of ministry opportunities, she made the decision to make my sister and me her priority. I doubt it was always glamorous to spend her time teaching us, playing with us and raising us in the church. But I do know that if you ask her today, she will tell you that she made the best decision for that season of her life. She has no regrets.

SIGNIFICANCE THROUGH INSIGNIFICANCE

The way Jesus operates is different from how the world operates. To Jesus, the way up is down—the way to significance is insignificance. Good shepherds are willing to leave the ninety-nine sheep to go after one individual lamb. Sound crazy? This is the way God works. The one individual is always important to God. Small acts of kindness are big to the person receiving them. Mother Teresa said it this way:

> It may happen that a mere smile, a short visit, the lighting of a lamp, writing a letter for a blind man, carrying a bucket of charcoal, offering a pair of sandals, reading the newspaper for someone—something small, very small—may, in fact, be our love of God in action.[2]

37

A young lady in our youth ministry at Generation Church was recently the recipient of one such act:

> When I moved to Washington from Arizona, I was a shy, nervous and uncomfortable seventh-grader sitting in the back row of the church. At the end of a service, I would run out, thankful for the escape. The next week, I would brace myself once again, preparing for the worst. A girl that I remembered meeting once or twice approached me with her familiar smile. Since there had been a lengthy time since our last meeting, I was surprised to find that she remembered my name. We talked and she began to include me in her circle of friends and activities, and we eventually became great friends. Because of her willingness to meet new people and make the effort to remember my name, I was able to break a fear barrier in my life, get more involved in church and meet new people. I am living proof that a smile and a friendly hello can really encourage someone's life.

This young lady is now an active part of Generation Church, reaching out to others and bringing friends from her school campus to the Lord. Just think of how many lives have been affected because one individual stepped out and said hello to a new person.

LITTLE BY LITTLE

Peter would not have responded to Jesus' call to launch out into the deep if he first had not been willing to launch out a little. I doubt Jesus would have led Peter to his miraculous catch if he had resisted the first command to launch out a little. The word "little" Jesus uses here refers to "few in number, multitude, effort or time."[3] God does not start by asking us to be Billy Graham and see 1.6 million people saved. He begins by asking us to put out a little bit of effort and time to touch a few people's lives. It's that simple.

This takes all of the pressure off. I can just be Judah Smith, a friendly student who cares for people. I still remember the day my neighbor came to church with me. To be honest, I wasn't trying to win him to Christ; I was just using his basketball hoop because mine had been damaged in a windstorm. I played varsity basketball for the local high school and he was in junior high, so I used my leverage to use his hoop and

39

play with him. We were having a fun time when I realized what time it was and that I needed to go. As I ran off, he asked, "Where are you going?"

I immediately replied, "Oh, you know, church." I had talked to him about church before but nothing ever really stuck—or so it seemed. He responded right back, "Can I come?" I stopped and said, "Yeah, sure, absolutely!" I was surprised. Even though I had prayed for him and talked to him about God, I was stunned that he asked me. I didn't realize that just playing basketball with him had really made a difference. He was now asking to go to church. Wow! That night my neighbor responded to the altar call and gave his life to Jesus.

I am afraid we have things backward too many times. Here's the point: In the Christian world, doing big events to reach people is vogue and makes headlines. But before you hold a rally to see your entire campus saved, why not start with loving one friend? Before you try to feed all the homeless people in your city, why not start by feeding one? Before you move to Africa to start an orphanage, take the neighbor kids whose parents just got a divorce to the local pizza place. If you don't launch out a little and touch the life of your neighbor, will you really be ready for the big event?

A PRAYERFUL PLACE

Lord, help me to see the value of what seems insignificant. I pray that You will guide me every day so that I don't overlook people or chances to minister to them. I thank You for daily opportunities to do little things with extravagant love. You haven't overwhelmed me with huge responsibility or expectation. You've asked me to be faithful with what is in front of me. Show me how to demonstrate Your love to my family, friends and classmates. Thank You for using every little opportunity in my life for Your glory.

41

Notes
1. Paul Lee Tan, *Encyclopedia of 7,700 Illustration* (Rockville, MD: Assurance Publishers, 1979).
2. Mother Teresa, *In the Heart of the World* (Novato, CA: New World Library, 1997), p. 39.
3. Bible Explorer, *Strong's Concordance* (Austin, TX: Epiphany Software, 1999), CD-ROM, s.v. "little."

4

THE CHALLENGE OF **CONFIDENCE** IN THE FACE OF FAILURE

I LOVED PLAYING BASKETBALL IN HIGH SCHOOL. One thing I had in abundance was confidence. My junior year, however, was the true test of that confidence. It seemed as though I made mistake after mistake. As a result, I started to play tentatively, I wouldn't go for my shots, my overall play was weak, and I wasn't really enjoying myself. Yet I still heard my dad's voice from the crowd: "Son, play with confidence." It wasn't easy, but I learned to look past my mistakes and remain confident.

After Jesus finished teaching the crowd of people in Luke 5, He went on to teach His soon-to-be disciples. The disciples had fished all night and caught nothing, yet Jesus commanded them to go back out into the deep. His words "launch out" infer confidence (verse 4). Nobody launches out into the deep without a certain level of confidence. Jesus was testing the confidence of His disciples.

Just as I struggled with my confidence in playing basketball, so too many Christians struggle with their confidence to be witnesses. Just as I was hesitant to launch a shot on the court, so too many of us hesitate to launch into someone's life to share the good news of Jesus Christ. Let me share another story that illustrates this point.

A CONFIDENT FREE FALL

44

I am sure many of you have been forced, as I was, to participate in a free fall at some youth event. Just in case you haven't, let me explain. Members of a team, one at a time, must climb up on a wooden pillar or other high point, close their eyes and fall straight back, trusting that their teammates will catch them.

I will never forget my experience at camp. We were told it was a test of trust. I've never understood exactly how that was supposed to teach us trust, but now that I'm a few years removed from this troubling experience, I can draw a few lessons from it. As I stepped up on the pillar, all I could think about was how much it would hurt if my junior high school friends didn't catch me. I stood there for what seemed like an eternity, asking over and over, "Are you sure you're going to catch me?"

"Yes!" they would all answer in unison. It wasn't until I was more confident than scared that I finally launched off the log into their arms.

Here is my point: Until we are more confident in God and His Word than we are scared for our own well-being and reputation, we will never launch into people's lives. Confidence is critical to our launching. We need to be as sure as the NASA space-shuttle controllers when they commence the launching of each shuttle. Our confidence in God commences the launching sequence of our life.

45

The disciples also had to choose whether they were going to respond in confidence or be paralyzed by their past failures. Jesus said, "Launch out" (Luke 5:4). Were the disciples going to base their responses on their previous results or were they going to have confidence in Jesus' word? This is the challenge of confidence in the face of failure. I believe this was Jesus' way of saying to each disciple, "Son, play with confidence."

THE BEST LIFE EVER

A few weeks ago, a 17-year-old girl shared her testimony with Generation Church, also referred to as

GC. She was faced with a decision: launch out despite her failure or allow past results to keep her stagnant. I hope her story moves you as much as it moved me:

> To my family, church always felt like more of a chore than a strong desire. My parents were raised in a strict Catholic environment, so the idea of shoving any type of religion down their children's throats didn't appeal to them. If and when we went to church, it was during the holidays or the occasional streak when my mom wanted to go. The day before, she would let us know that she was going to church and would give us the option of going with her. I always went because I liked dressing up. The very few times we did go to a Sunday service, we always went to a different church. I don't think we ever went to the same church twice, which made me think that church was an unwelcoming place where I didn't know anybody.
>
> My parents raised me to believe whatever I wanted. They didn't know what they believed, and they didn't want to teach me the wrong thing. Since I didn't know the truth

of God's Word growing up, I concluded that by being a good person and doing the right things—not killing anybody or doing anything too extreme—I would have my ticket to heaven.

I was always a good kid, got good grades, had a good attitude about life and was all around pretty normal. In second grade, I skipped a grade and started hanging out with older kids. By seventh grade, most of my friends were in high school, and during the summer between seventh and eighth grade, I smoked weed for the first time. Once I hit high school, I turned into a party animal! All my friends and I would get drunk and smoke weed—this was normal activity at my school. My parents never knew I was doing these things. By my junior year, I was smoking weed two or three times a week and all weekend long. My grades were still good and I hadn't killed anybody, so I figured I still had my ticket into those pearly gates.

At the beginning of my senior year, two of my closest friends who I used to party with invited me to Generation Church. I was actually excited. I mainly wanted to go

47

because I was interested in the message. I liked the fact that the church was so relaxed and you could be yourself. I actually felt welcomed! I started to go regularly. On September 19, 2001, I responded to an altar call for salvation and accepted Jesus Christ as my Lord and Savior! Immediately, I plugged into a cadre and began to learn about God, the Bible and how I needed to change my lifestyle. Slowly but surely, I put down the drugs and alcohol, tried to stop swearing and was on fire for God. At the time, I think I jumped into everything so fast—wanting to be as dedicated as my close friends—that I didn't realize the depth of the commitment I had made. I loved GC and wanted to share it with so many people. I invited everyone I could think of, and pretty soon, GC turned into a social event. Eventually two pews of friends from school came to hang out with us on Wednesday night. I was in the right place but for the wrong reasons. I began to lose sight of God.

By April of my senior year, I walked away from God. I didn't just fall back into my old ways; I hit rock bottom. Before I accepted

Christ, I was smoking and drinking occasionally. Now it was all the time. On April 15, 2002, my seventeenth birthday, I wanted to do weed again. I smoked a bowl with my friends and we swore not to tell anybody. Soon our sessions became more and more frequent, and everybody knew about my habit. I was close friends with the drug dealers and stoners. It got so bad that I literally smoked throughout the day.

On July 7, God stepped in to help me in a way I wouldn't have expected. Six of my friends and I went to the lake to do drugs. As soon as I took a hit, a flashlight temporarily blinded my sight and the word "freeze" stopped my heart. Some more of my friends were supposed to meet us, so I thought it was just them messing around. I was wrong. It was a police officer. We were immediately arrested and taken to the police station. As soon as the police called my parents, I was in big trouble. That night, I confessed all of the lies to my parents. I didn't care about hiding anymore. I had been caught red-handed and decided to tell them everything they never knew. As strange

49

as it may sound, getting arrested was one of the best things to ever happen to me.

As a result of telling my parents everything, I was no longer allowed to hang out with certain friends. This left me with my two close friends from church. I started going back to church on Wednesday nights, but just to get out of the house and hear the message, not to receive it. Then, one night, God broke my heart. I rededicated my life in August 2002 and have been on fire for God ever since! I know the lies and deceit of the enemy, and I pray that I will walk with God all the days of my life. It is not my life to live. I want to live according to God's plan, because I know He can give me the best life ever!

We can learn many lessons from this young lady's testimony. When she started going back to church, she had a hard decision to make: put her confidence in something that didn't seem to work the first time or put her trust in God alone. Even though she had seemingly failed in her relationship with God the first time, she tried again and rededicated her life to Christ.

There are three important keys that give us the ability to overcome challenges in the midst of failure. You may find yourself agreeing with everything that has been written to this point, but in the back of your mind a little voice says, *I have tried all this before. I know it's the right thing to do, but reaching people just doesn't work for me.* If this is true, you need to start exercising the following three principles in order to overcome your doubt and lack of confidence:

1. *Christ is our confidence*: Proverbs 3:26 says, "For the Lord will be your confidence and will keep your foot from being snared" (*NIV*). As you step out in obedience to the Lord and His Word, you must put your trust in Him. He will keep you from stumbling.

2. *Our confidence is not based on results*: Sometimes results will be as we expect, while at other times we won't see any. "Faith is being sure of what we hope for and certain of what we do not see" (Hebrews 11:1, *NIV*). If we only have confidence when we see tangible results, we are not truly living the life of faith. God knows that at times we will be tempted to lose confidence if

the results aren't as we anticipate; therefore, He encourages, "Therefore do not cast away your confidence, which has great reward" (10:35). We will get a reward when we persevere beyond what we see.

3. *Confidence is not the denial of failure:* True confidence isn't acting like you never fail or mess up (that's called denial). The confidence that comes through Christ enables you to put failure in its proper place. If you have failed due to your own sin, you can be set free from condemnation through the work of the cross (see Romans 8:1). If you seem to have failed when you stepped out in obedience to God's Word, you have to trust that He is in control and working all things together for good (see verse 28).

Overcoming the challenge of confidence in the face of failure is one of the biggest lessons of faith we encounter in life. Once we overcome and have a confidence based on Christ, we are ready to launch out into the deep and go to places we have never gone before.

A PRAYERFUL PLACE

God, I thank You that I live by what You say and not by immediate results. Help me to walk by faith, knowing that You will accomplish what You sent me to do. I trust that my labor of love is not in vain and I will reap what I sow if I do not lose heart. You're a rewarder of diligence and faithfulness. Lord, I pray that You would reward my obedience to Your Word with the salvation of my friends. Father, You know the areas where I have lost my confidence. I pray that You will restore to me a new trust in You. I desire the reward that comes from this confidence in You.

53

5

THE CHALLENGE OF **CONSTANCY** IN THE MIDST OF UNFRUITFULNESS

I KNEW I HAD SOMETHING BIG ON THE OTHER END OF MY FISHING LINE. I was so excited I could hardly contain myself. I tugged and pulled until my pole was bending under the pressure of the imminent large catch I was reeling in. This had to be a huge fish.

I could already visualize the picture-perfect moment. As I whipped the catch out of the water, my excitement turned to embarrassment. My prized catch was a huge ball of seaweed. I couldn't believe it. All that work for seaweed.

Many times our efforts to reach people seem to be in vain—like catching a ball of seaweed. Have you ever invited your neighbors to church or finally mustered up enough courage to share Christ with a friend only to have them walk away? What do you do? How do you respond when you have fished all day and night and your net is empty? What do you do when your ministry, business, school or home life doesn't seem to be making a difference in anyone's life?

KEEP THE LINE IN THE WATER

Great fishermen face discouragement at times, but they conquer it. Similarly, you will experience seasons when your net is empty, but they won't last long. The key to responding properly during these times is not to allow discouragement to determine your response.

There are times in life when it seems that everything God has spoken is on hold—times of vision without the realization of that vision. Maybe you are a businessperson with a dream of employing hundreds and sharing Christ with each one. Maybe your vision is to go to the mission field and build an orphanage to house children and teach them about the love of God. Waiting for the fulfillment of the vision is the time when you must trust God and walk by faith.

It is in these seasons that true fishermen are proven—they are tested by time. Ask any avid fisherman and he will tell you that one of the key characteristics of a successful fisherman is patience.

Some days you just have to wait and keep your line in the water.

Keeping your line in the water means that if your friend doesn't get saved the first time you witness to him or her, continue to tell your friend about Jesus. It means that even if you don't feel like sharing the gospel, you still need to do it. This takes endurance! God says, "For you have need of endurance, so that after you have done the will of God, you may receive the promise" (Hebrews 10:36).

Amy, one of Generation Church's amazing cadre leaders, kept her line in the water even when it seemed unfruitful. She didn't give up on a girl named Breanna. This is Breanna's story:

> I had been in church my entire life but never really knew who God was. I met one of the leaders of Generation Church on my high school campus. She was full of life and very excited to meet me. This encounter turned into an amazing friendship.
>
> After the initial meeting, Amy called me once a week, on Sunday afternoon, and invited me to come to her cadre. Honestly, I didn't want to go, but my good churchgoing self didn't want to hurt her feelings. I

would entertain the idea but never show up. Even in my absence, Amy remained consistent. She always called, always had a great attitude and never looked down on me for not showing up.

This cycle continued for about four months, and then the phone calls didn't come quite as often. Yet when I did hear from Amy it was refreshing. It showed me that someone really did care about me. Amy wasn't flaky like most people I knew; she was faithful and sincere. Something began to stir inside me about why she cared about me, so I decided to go to her small group. She even took me out to dinner and coffee to talk about things I was dealing with and questions I had.

I had never met someone quite like Amy. Even better, I had never met anyone like the One she introduced me to, Jesus Christ. Because of Amy's faithfulness and faith, I am serving God today. She displayed a love greater than the world had to offer. She laid down her life for a friend, which is the greatest love of all. I know I am forever changed because of her investment in my life.

Today Breanna is an amazing cadre leader. She has put into practice the same kind of constancy with the young ladies in her cadre that Amy demonstrated to her. In fact, one of Breanna's ministries at GC is to make a list of all the young people who have missed GC three weeks in a row. Every week she leaves the list on my desk and my wife and I call each one of them. Little did Amy know that her constancy and patience would affect so many lives.

DECLARE JESUS AS THE CAPTAIN OF YOUR SHIP

We often experience empty nets, just as Peter did. But we see that Peter responded to Christ in such a way that a great catch of fish followed. When Peter called Jesus "Master" (Luke 5:5), he demonstrated who was in charge of his boat. He was not afraid to be honest about the circumstances—no fish—and he also recognized who was in charge.

Unless Jesus is the captain of our ship, we can fish all day and night without seeing any results. The harvest is on God's terms, not ours. This means it is according to His timing, His methods and ultimately His responsibility. Our job is simply to obey. Unless we completely turn our ship over to

Christ, we will never experience the great harvest God has appointed to us.

DON'T TOIL IN VAIN

As we look at Peter's response to Jesus, we gain another insight into the kind of work he had been doing all night. Peter used the word "toiled" (Luke 5:5), which represents work that we do by our own efforts, abilities and strategies. We can toil and work until we are exhausted, but without God and His divine hand in our fishing endeavors, our nets will remain empty.

We must actively guard against switching into a default mode of trying to save people by our own strength or persuasive words. This will ultimately leave us exhausted and burned out. The book of Psalms cautions us:

> It is vain for you to rise up early, to sit up late, to eat the bread of sorrows; for so He gives His beloved sleep (127:2).

It is worthless for us to stay up all night or get up early to try to work things out by our own strength. If God asks us to stay up all night fishing, we obey and His grace enables us. But if God hasn't told us so, then we are working in vain.

The disciples had worked all night and caught nothing because they were working in their own strength based on their own understanding. To truly see our homes, schools, workplaces and cities won for Christ, we cannot lean on our own experiences or abilities. We must trust God to use us, direct us and show us how to reach people.

A PRAYERFUL PLACE

God, I thank You that I walk by faith and not by sight. Thank You for the endurance to press on. I pray that You would help me to keep my eyes on You, knowing that You are faithful to Your promises. You are the master in charge of my life, and I pray that You will help me to keep obeying Your Word even when I don't see immediate results.

God, I trust Your timing and Your methods. I will not toil in my own ability; instead, I will obey You and trust Your results. I trust You to take the seeds that I have planted and cause them to grow. You're the One who draws people to You. I trust You to bring forth fruitfulness through my obedience.

61

6

THE CHALLENGE OF **CONTENDING** IN UNCHARTED TERRITORY

WHEN JESUS ASKED THE DISCIPLES TO LAUNCH OUT INTO THE DEEP, HE WAS ASKING THEM TO GO INTO UNCHARTED TERRITORY. Because Peter and his crew were professional fishermen, they knew that the best catch was usually found in the shallower part of the lake. Around twilight the fish would swim closer to the surface of the water to eat; therefore, the fishermen would fish at night. Jesus was asking Peter to do something new. He asked Peter to step out in confidence and go fishing where he wasn't used to fishing.

Once you put your confidence in Christ, you position yourself to go fishing for souls in places you have never gone before. Up to this point, Jesus had taught lessons to the disciples about growing in compassion, making sure they weren't isolated, caring about the seemingly insignificant, and placing their confidence in Christ. Christ was now ready to call the disciples to a greater level of sacrifice.

GREATER FAITH, DISCIPLINE AND DEDICATION

Fishing in deep water is more demanding than launching out a little. It requires more faith, discipline and dedication. To fish in deep water, we can no longer rely on our own strength, efforts or previous knowledge of fishing. It's a whole new way of living. It is only in the deep water, trusting completely on God's Word, that the supernatural takes place. The benefit is worth the investment.

"Expect great things; attempt great things."[1] This is a famous quote by William Carey, the father of modern Protestant missions. At the beginning of Carey's ministry in the late eighteenth century, he appealed to a board of leaders to place more value on overseas missions. One of the leaders abruptly interrupted him, saying, "Young man, sit down! You are an enthusiast. When God pleases to convert the heathen, He'll do it without consulting you or me."[2] Even though missions and evangelism were not as important to the Church during those days, Carey was determined to live out the Great Commission, insisting that it applied to all Christians of all times.

In 1792, Carey organized a missionary society. By 1793, he had formed a team to evangelize the nation of India. It would be a lie to say that life was easy for Carey after that decision. While in India, team members left him, his five-year-old son died, and his wife's mental health deteriorated.

Finally, after seven years on the mission field, Carey baptized his first convert. Seven years! We think we've failed if nobody is saved after a month. Two months after baptizing his first convert, Carey published his first Bengali New Testament. Over the next twenty-eight years, he translated the entire Bible and opened up doors for the Bible to be published in many other languages and dialects.

By the time William Carey died, he had spent forty-one years in India without ever returning home. His mission work saw seven hundred people saved, and he laid a foundation for many other missionaries to evangelize effectively in that nation.

The greatest legacy William Carey left was the inspiration for the worldwide missions movement. His work inspired missionaries such as Hudson Taylor and David Livingston. Because this man was willing to launch out into the deep, many people

65

followed his example and expected great things and attempted great things.

HOUSE PARTY

Launching out into the deep doesn't necessarily imply going to the mission field. God has a specific plan and destiny for each individual to launch out into the deep. This may mean a new way of reaching people on your campus or workplace. If you are a youth pastor, God may be calling you to seek Him in prayer for a new strategy to evangelize your city.

At Generation Church, we believe that God is saving more young people on campuses. Throughout the years, we have had faithful students who have launched Bible studies, prayer by the flagpole, pizza feeds and after-school rallies. Through these methods, we have seen many young people saved, but we haven't seen a supernatural catch from launching out into the deep. Therefore, we have initiated what we call "house parties."

I wish we could say that we prayed, fasted and sought God, and then He gave us a supernatural revelation, but the idea of house parties just fell into our laps. A group of students from a local high school wanted to see their friends saved, but their

Bible study wasn't happening. They came to us one day and asked if they could have a house party, sponsored by the church, with the intention of sharing the gospel with their unsaved friends. We felt good about it, had funds in our budget to buy pizza, and went for it.

After two house parties (we couldn't think of a better name), fifty students had attended, mostly unsaved, and heard the good news of Jesus Christ. Within a few months, six people were saved, were planted in Generation Church, and were growing in Christ. To be honest, this was more people than had been saved and planted in church from any campus Bible study, so we decided to try another house party.

In January 2003, GC launched its first house party at the University of Washington. A Baptist fraternity on Greek row offered to let us use their house to minister to the campus. (Talk about community partnership!) Two University of Washington students planned the entire party, GC paid for it, and together we launched out into the deep.

Around two hundred students (only fifteen were GC leaders) came to a Christian atmosphere, heard about Generation Church, listened to testimonies from our leaders, and absolutely loved it.

67

Nobody complained that there weren't any drugs, alcohol or dancing. One young man told me, "This is the best party I've ever been to! Every weekend I go to parties with alcohol and girls in tank tops and miniskirts; big deal, it gets old. But this is different! People are happy. The girls are classy. If you have this party every weekend, I'll bring all my friends."

Consequently, quite a few of those students have visited Generation Church, and two have been saved and are being discipled.

We have moved out into our city's school campuses based on God's Word. The only way to be successful at launching into the deep is through a word from God. Peter didn't assume, *Hey, Jesus is in my boat. I heard that He does supernatural things. Maybe I should go out into the deep.* Instead, Peter waited for a word from God. We will address this more in a few chapters, but I want to take time now to caution you: Don't launch out into the deep based on assumption. Always make sure that you have the approval of your parents, youth pastor and/or senior pastor. To go places you have never gone before, you need the protection of authority. God always works through the authority He places in your life.

As we launch out into the deep based on God's Word, with the protection of authority, we are on our way to experiencing a supernatural catch of fish. After all, God desires that all men and women will be saved even more than you do!

A PRAYERFUL PLACE

Lord, I'm so thankful that You came and did what You did when it didn't make sense to the people around You. I pray that You would put it in my heart to obey You and go where I have not gone before. I ask that You would give me the mind of Christ to know how to be effective not only in the little things but also in the big things, even if others may not have attempted it before. I pray that You would show me what to do, what sacrifices to make and how to prepare for things far beyond my own ability.

69

God, I ask that You would speak to me and to my youth pastor, parents and even my friends, giving us strategies to reach more people effectively. I pray that doors would open on my campus to speak up about You and make Your name great. God, I believe that You will speak to me, and when You do, You will help me to obey quickly.

Notes

1. Mark Galli, comp., *131 Christians Everyone Should Know* (Nashville, TN: Broadman and Holman, 2000), p. 246.
2. Ibid., p. 244.

70

7

THE CHALLENGE OF **CONTRITENESS** OF HEART

HAVE YOU EVER HAD WHAT SEEMED LIKE A GREAT STRATEGY FOR REACHING A HURTING WORLD THAT YOU THOUGHT WAS FROM GOD, BUT WHEN IT CAME DOWN TO IT, YOU DIDN'T EXPERIENCE THE HARVEST YOU EXPECTED? As a youth pastor, I have often wondered why some outreaches don't seem to reach anyone. I would like to propose to you that often it has to do with the position of our nets. Unless we lower our nets to the level that people are at, our efforts to reach them will be limited.

Many times during my preaching preparation, the Holy Spirit has stopped me and questioned my motives: Was I preparing to preach for the applause of Christians or the transformation of human lives? Was I operating from pride or love for people?

Once we launch out into the deep and begin to experience God's supernatural catch of fish, we must revisit the issue of motive that we discussed in chapter 1. It's easy to be motivated by a pure love for people when we do seemingly insignificant acts. The challenge of humility comes when we begin to reach multitudes: Are we willing to humble ourselves, let down our nets and do whatever it takes to meet people where they are at?

One of the greatest role models for reaching people is Mother Teresa. Even while she was reaching multitudes in Calcutta, India, she was never afraid to let down her nets as low as it took to reach the individual. This is her story of ministering to one particular man:

72

Some of my sisters work in Australia. On a reservation, among the Aborigines, there was an elderly man. I can assure you that you have never seen a situation as difficult as that poor old man's. He was completely ignored by everyone. His home was disordered and dirty.

I told him, "Please, let me clean your house, wash your clothes, and make your bed." He answered, "I'm okay like this. Let it be."

I said again, "You will be better if you allow me to do it."

He finally agreed. So I was able to clean his house and wash his clothes. I discovered a beautiful lamp, covered with dust. Only God knows how many years had passed since he last lit it.

I said to him, "Don't you light your lamp? Don't you ever use it?"

He answered, "No. No one comes to see me. I have no need to light it. Who would I light it for?"

I asked, "Would you come to light it if the sisters came?"

He replied, "Of course."

From that day on, the sisters committed themselves to visiting him every evening. We cleaned the lamp, and the sisters would light it every evening.

Two years passed. I had completely forgotten that man. He sent this message: "Tell my friend that the light she lit in my life continues to shine still."[1]

This testimony of great humility had an impact on me. In fact, its simplicity makes it so remarkable. Mother Teresa's willingness to do the simple acts of kindness is a reflection of her humility.

We also must possess the willingness to commit ourselves to the simple acts of caring for people. These acts of caring may not appear to be historic or noteworthy, but they work into us a deeper humility as we meet the needs of people. Simple acts of caring for the real needs of real people make up a daily lifestyle of the truly great people-reachers. If we expect our daily life to be a continuum of big events, we will grow disillusioned. We will stop relating to the individual and letting down our nets to a level where people can be reached.

BROKENNESS

Psalm 51:17 gives us a glimpse into what pleases God: "The sacrifices of God are a broken spirit; a broken and a contrite heart, O God, you will not despise" (*NIV*). The word "contrite" means "crushed" or "broken."[2] This doesn't mean that God literally wants to crush our heart; it means that God wants to change our attitude and spirit. Our selfish desires and motives must be crushed so that God may form in us His desires and passions. Psalm 51:17 indicates that God's most desired sacrifice is a humble and broken heart that we place in His hands to be rebuilt by Him.

This kind of heart is forged only through a genuine relationship with God. I am not talking about a false show of humility or a self-imposed condemnation, but rather an honest recognition of who we are and who God is. Humility is actually the source of healthy, authentic self-confidence because we base our value and identity on Jesus rather than on our works. As we come to know Jesus more, our selfish desires and habits begin to lose their hold on us. Our hearts become soft, pliable and responsive to Him.

I can't explain it, but when I pray, "Not my will, but Your will be done," a supernatural exchange takes place. He gives me His strength for my weakness. He gives me His righteousness for my unrighteousness. He gives me His pure desires for my selfish desires.

A PRAYERFUL PLACE

Father, I pray that You would search my heart and remove any prideful desire to impress people rather than to reach them. I don't want to make my reputation with Christians more important than my purpose in You. Help me, Lord, to be motivated out of sincere love and care for people. I don't want to

witness in order to show people that I'm a good
Christian or to make myself feel as if I've fulfilled
some religious duty. I need Your pure love.

Please show me how to simply care for people
and be a servant to everyone. Remind me where I
come from and keep me humble and close to You.
God, I recognize that I wouldn't be where
I am today without Your incredible gift of grace.
Create in me a clean heart and give me a contrite
spirit. Help me to show the same love for people
that You show to me.

Notes
1. Mother Teresa, *In the Heart of the World* (Novato, CA: New World Library, 1997), pp. 53-54.
2. Bible Explorer, *Strong's Concordance* (Austin, TX: Epiphany Software, 1999), CD-ROM, s.v. "contrite."

8

THE CHALLENGE OF CHRIST'S **COMMANDMENTS** DETERMINING OUR ACTION

I SAT IN MY CAR THAT MORNING WONDERING IF I COULD REALLY DO IT. My heart was pounding; I couldn't believe I had told everyone I was going to stand up and preach in my high school lunchroom. I started to reason in my mind, *Maybe this isn't the best day. Yeah, I should probably wait. What will my friends think anyway?* It was the first lunch period of my senior year and everybody in the entire school was having lunch together. Could I really do it? Doubt and fear were moving in for the kill.

I desperately grabbed my big, blue Bible out of my bag and asked God to speak to me. Not knowing where to turn, I did what any great man or woman of God would do. I closed my eyes, flipped open the pages and pointed to a passage. I didn't really expect God to speak to me, but I thought it couldn't hurt. I looked down and read these words:

"In Judah God is known" (Psalm 76:1, *NIV*). I was amazed. God spoke to me. At that moment, my fear was eliminated.

Minutes later I was standing in the Issaquah High School cafeteria with nearly a thousand of my fellow students. My sister Wendy, Pastor Jude Fouquier and Pastor Steve Carpenter came to support me. My friend Jordan asked me if I wanted to walk around and talk to people. I replied, "No, there is something I have to do." Knowing what I was planning, he gasped, "Oh man!" and quickly sat back down.

I stood up on my chair and began shouting, "Excuse me! Can I have your attention, please?" Everybody stopped and stared at me. I had to keep going: "My name is Judah. Some of you probably know me from the basketball team, but what many of you may not know is that I am a Christian. Some of you are probably wondering if Jesus Christ is real. I am here to tell you that He is real and He changed my life." I continued sharing some of my testimony and two sophomores got up to leave. I shouted to them, "You need to stay and hear this! Besides, I'm bigger than you!" They quickly sat down.

About halfway through my testimony, a few of my classmates began clapping and, as a result, some students had a hard time hearing me. Glen, the captain of the football team, stood up and shouted, "Be quiet! He isn't finished." They were quiet.

As I finished my testimony, I invited everybody to my campus Bible study. I couldn't believe I actually did it! I know full well that without the word God spoke to me from Psalm 76, I wouldn't have been able to speak out in my high school cafeteria. When the odds are against you and fear or failure is trying to hold you back, the Word of God will motivate you. Peter didn't want to return to the lake where he had fished all night without results, but he went because God spoke to him. I preached in my lunchroom because God spoke to me. By the end of my senior year, many of my classmates received Jesus Christ as their Lord and Savior, all because God spoke to me and I obeyed His lead.

STOCKED PONDS

As we launch out into the deep to reach more people, we must depend on the Word of God to direct us to good fishing holes. He knows where the fish are.

As a little boy, I loved to go fishing with my dad. We would get up at three in the morning and drive to Rainbow Lake with our neighbors. One morning we caught twenty-eight rainbow trout. I thought we were the best fishermen ever. Later, I found out that I just have a smart dad who took me to a stocked pond full of fish waiting to be caught. In the same way, God knows where there are people just waiting to receive Him.

If we will draw close to God and let Him direct our fishing, He will lead us to strategic areas where people are ready to be saved. The challenge is waiting for His lead. It is easy to look at what other Christians are doing and feel pressured into doing something great for God based on our own strength and knowledge. Yet to be effective in loving and reaching people, we must trust God and wait for His direction.

There really are different ways to fish for people. One method is to grab your pole and start casting with no discernment or awareness of people's needs or the readiness of their hearts to hear your words. Another method involves scouting: waiting and preparing based on a word from God. At times this method appears much slower, but the truth is that it produces larger and more worthwhile catches.

Among the staff members at our church, we have a longstanding joke that our church only has two speeds: wait and go fast. These two speeds come

CHRIST'S **COMMANDMENTS** DETERMINING OUR ACTION

from the method of fishing that has been estab-
lished by my mom and dad, the pastors of City
Church. At City Church, we pray and wait and pray
some more. When God tells us where to cast our
line, we grab our poles and go fast! After ten years
of growth, City Church and its youth congrega-
tion—Generation Church—are great examples of
fishing based on a word from God.

There are stocked ponds in each of our cities,
communities, businesses, neighborhoods and
schools. We simply need to be willing to wait to
hear God's direction. As we do this, God can position us to reach entire cities.

81

A PRAYERFUL PLACE

Father, I thank You that You've given me ears to
hear what You're saying to me. I pray that You will
keep me in Your Word and that You will bring
Scriptures to my mind. Your Word renews my mind
so that I will know Your perfect will and plan for me.
I ask that You will help me to never do anything
apart from a word from You.

Help me to wait on You so that I can hear clearly
without confusion. Your Word will move me beyond

fear or doubt. I need Your Word in order to do what
You have called me to do. I trust You to lead me to
people who want to meet You. I believe that
You will use my obedience. Thank You for revealing
Your purpose that You have prepared for me.

Judah Smith

9

THE CHALLENGE OF **CITYWIDE** THINKING AND INFLUENCE

MY THINKING IS TOO SMALL. I ADMIT IT! I HAVE LIMITED GOD FAR TOO OFTEN. I thought my vision of having thousands participate in our youth church was His ultimate vision for my life. I was wrong. God's vision is much larger. God wants my entire city!

Within a 30-mile radius of our church building in Kirkland, Washington, there are 130,000 young people between the ages of 12 and 24. Chances are that most of them are probably not Christians. We have our job cut out for us. My vision for our youth church must include reaching these young people—all of them.

Of course, we can't do this alone. We will work alongside other churches in our area. Together we will go after each one of these young people.

The Bible tells us that God desires all men to be saved (see 1 Timothy 2:4). That means everyone! If we operate by our natural mind, it is easy to doubt how this can happen.

ENLARGE YOUR THINKING

During a special meeting with Dr. Marilyn Hickey at City Church, she stopped preaching, laid her hands on me and said, "Your thinking is too small. It's too small. God wants to enlarge your thinking!"

To be honest with you, I was more than a little surprised. I thought my vision of a youth church of thousands was rather impressive. Again, I was wrong. Our God is the God of Abraham, the One who told Abraham that his descendants would be like the innumerable stars and the endless sand of the seashore (see Genesis 22:17). Have you ever tried to count a handful of sand?

If God told you to reach 5,000 people, would you believe that He could give you that number? How about 50,000 or 500,000? My thinking has been enlarged and is being enlarged. How about yours?

Not long ago at City Church, we had the privilege of hosting Dr. David Yonggi Cho. When you hear a man of his faith speak, you begin to realize how small your own thinking is. Dr. Cho chose to believe God for growth to more than 800,000 members in his church. What's the point? God wants us to think bigger. More people need to get saved and get added to the Church. Our churches need to get bigger.

Dr. Cho tells the story of how God took him through a process of enlarging his vision for more people. In the early years of his church, when he only had 500 members, he believed for church growth to 3,000. God told him, "When you can see 3,000 church members in your heart, come and ask me and I will fulfill it."[1] Dr. Cho continues the story:

> So I was praying day in and day out for 3,000 people, and soon I could dream the church was full of 3,000 members, and I could communicate this with the Holy Spirit. I was praising the Lord and I had clear visions and dreams of the church with 3,000. Soon I was preaching as if I was preaching to 3,000 people even though there were only 500 members. People would come up to me and say, "Pastor, you only have 500 people, don't shout too hard because we have pain in our ears."
>
> But I said, "No, I'm speaking to 3,000 people. God calls those things that are not as though they were." So I was talking as if

I had 3,000 members; I was dreaming as if I already had 3,000; I was rejoicing as if I had 3,000; and I was living as if I were the pastor of 3,000. By 1964, I had 3,000. So you see, what you can see you can have.[2]

PACK OUT THE HOUSE

We see this principle in Luke 5:6: God wants more people saved! He uses the illustration of the boat filled with a great number of fish to demonstrate that He wants our churches filled with people. God wants great numbers, because numbers represent people. To Jesus, each person is an eternal soul that He died for and had in mind on the cross. It would be strange for us to not rejoice when we see the fulfillment of God's purposes when more people are added to the Church. Our God wants a packed house.

When Jesus told the parable of the great supper, He illustrated God's desire for His house to be filled: "And the lord said unto the servant, Go out into the highways and hedges, and compel them to come in, that my house may be filled" (Luke 14:23). We need to clearly understand that our Lord and Savior didn't die for a select few but for all humankind. With this revelation, it is now our responsibility, empowered by the Holy Spirit, to share the good news and believe for all men to be saved. Thus, our thinking and influence must be enlarged.

RENOVATE YOUR MIND

How does this enlarging take place? How was I supposed to respond to Dr. Marilyn Hickey's prophetic challenge over my life? One of the best ways to be enlarged in our minds is through the Bible. Just as we discussed in chapter 8, it is God's Word that is to direct our action. God's perfect Word is also supposed to dominate our thinking. The most effective way to enlarge our thinking and spiritual perspective is to devour the Word of God. As we read it on a daily basis, it renews our thought processes. As we read and study God's Word, our mind is literally renovated. Wrong thinking is removed and replaced with God's ideas and thoughts. As the renovation takes place, our thinking is changed and comes into alignment with God's thoughts.

I would like to take this moment to challenge a new generation of preachers and leaders in the Body of Christ. As the winds of doctrine blow and ideas about the end of the world loom large, we

87

must be a generation of the Word. The infallible, inerrant Word of God must be the bedrock of the emerging generation. If God's Word is not the anchor of our daily life and ministry, then we will not endure. We must allow ourselves to be forged and fashioned by God's Word. Only then can we become the end-time, formidable weapon God is calling for. Young person, youth pastor or parent, please don't settle for anything less than God's trustworthy and time-tested Word.

BELIEVE AND OBEY

Let's look again at Luke 5:6: "And when they had done this, they caught a great number of fish, and their net was breaking." This little verse gives us a secret to a great catch: "when they had done this." In other words, when they had responded to God's initiative. When we do what God wants us to do, great things happen. Our role is to discern what God is doing and get on board. He desires that everyone be saved, and if we are willing to respond to His direction, He would love for us to participate in loving and helping people everywhere.

Great trust and obedience precede great numbers. Just ask Abraham. He obeyed God to the point of being willing to sacrifice his son Isaac, and God promised to bless him and multiply his descendants. We must incorporate a total, immediate, obedient response to the Word of God into every aspect of our life. We need to both believe—trust God—and obey His commands with all our strength. If we step out, we will see that our faith and obedience will work together to produce a great harvest of people.

BELIEVE THE DREAM

As we conclude this chapter, I want to exhort you in the same way my father has exhorted our entire church: Believe the dream! This has become the theme of City Church. It comes from Genesis 15, where God reveals to Abraham His dream. God takes Abraham outside his tent and declares that his descendants will be like the innumerable stars. This is God's dream and we are Abraham's descendants. A great number of people are going to come through us into the kingdom of God. I regularly tell our young people that we will never apologize for praying and proclaiming for the thousands coming to Generation Church. This is the dream of my God. I encourage you by the Holy Spirit to believe God's dream for your city!

89

A PRAYERFUL PLACE

*God, forgive me for thinking too small. Please enlarge
my thinking. Give me a faith capacity to believe the
dream that You have for my city.*

*I pray that as I read and meditate on Your Word,
my faith will be challenged and You will give
me vision beyond natural possibilities. You are the
God of the impossible. Help me to see beyond the
context of my abilities to the endless possibilities in
You. Don't let my thinking limit what You want to do
through me in my city. Let Your will be done in my
life, in my family and in my city.*

90

Notes
P. Y. Cho, "How Churches Grow" (sermon, The City Church, Kirkland,
WA, May 6, 2002).
2. Ibid.

Judah Smith

10

THE CHALLENGE OF **COMMUNITY** PARTNERSHIP

GOD HAS CALLED US TO CATCH A GREAT NUMBER OF FISH AND REACH ENTIRE CITIES, BUT WE CAN'T DO IT ALONE! As the pastor of Generation Church, it would be overwhelming to attempt to reach the 130,000 young people in our area with only our church. But as we see in Luke 5:7, Jesus desires that we partner or team together with others in our community.

Jesus knew the great number of fish Peter was going to catch, so why didn't He instruct Peter to bring a larger net and boat? I think Jesus used this opportunity to teach His disciples and us the principle of community partnership. The word "partners" used in Luke 5:7 refers to "sharing in something together."[1] Is anybody sharing in your life with you?

Often while ministering, I encounter young people who tell me about their dreams of winning the lost, ministering to the broken or going to nations. Their desire is sincere and commendable, but in many cases they have yet to discover the principle of partnership. When that seems to be the case, I encourage them to get involved with the team in their local church and from there allow God to open doors of ministry. Ministry is always a team effort.

A PLACE OF VULNERABILITY

The risk of having partners is that they will see our weaknesses. Peter needed partners because he had a weakness in his net. Without partners, Peter might have hidden the weak point in his net, and then he wouldn't have caught the great number of fish. We must be willing to let other people share in our lives and strengthen our weaknesses in order to catch a great number of people.

Proverbs 18:1 instructs us, "A man who isolates himself seeks his own desire; he rages against all wise judgment." In other words, he isolates himself in order to do what he wants and also so that others can't give him input.

Instead of isolating ourselves, we need to establish partnerships. Setting up partnerships doesn't mean that we just attend a church and a small

92

group; it implies that we actively involve ourselves with people we can call when we need help. Peter wasn't afraid to shout across the lake to his partners when his net was breaking. We also must be willing to be vulnerable and ask for help.

A PLACE OF GATHERING

Each one of us needs to be committed and involved in a strong local church for the sake of our own spiritual growth. We also need a strong local church for the sake of people we will lead to Christ. Through the anointing that takes place in the corporate gathering of our local church, God will put us into contact with these people whom we otherwise could not reach. The following story is a powerful demonstration of this principle:

93

> My entire life I was searching for love. The love I found from men, friends and family seemed to fill me up but only for a season. My parents were refugees from Vietnam and came to America in 1980. I was born in 1983. Growing up, I was influenced by my Buddhist mother, and my father went along with whatever religion my mother wanted.

When I was in seventh grade, my mother's best friend led her to Christ, and she accepted Jesus Christ as her Lord and Savior. She wanted the same joy for my life, so I was baptized at the local Catholic church. The problem was that I wasn't changed on the inside. In fact, right after I was baptized, I snuck out of the service to hang with the stoners behind the church. I hated church. I thought all church people were ugly and stupid and had nothing better to do than worship some guy on a stick.

The next few years of my life I made some really bad decisions. I wanted love so badly that I hung out with all the wrong friends. I had a boyfriend who told me he loved me, but his love wasn't sincere. I started struggling with depression and attempted suicide many times. Life seemed worthless to me because nothing satisfied me. From the outside, you would probably think I had everything together, but deep down I was empty.

Toward the end of my sophomore year in high school, my father, frustrated with my friends, decided to move the family to the east side of Seattle. We moved to Red-mond, and I hated life even more. A month after we moved, my mother was diagnosed with cancer. She had had cancer earlier in life, but she had recovered. To be honest, I wasn't worried about her at all. I knew she would recover.

I didn't like Redmond High School, but eventually I made a few friends. After school one day, one of my friends dragged me to meet some guy who led a Bible study. She only wanted me to meet him because she thought he was good-looking, not because we had any interest in church! When I met him, I was shocked. This guy didn't fit my idea of Christians at all. He was friendly, smart and good-looking. There was some-thing different about this guy. He was not what I expected.

That very week, my mom checked into the hospital because her cancer was so bad. I confided in the young man from the Bible study and he went to the hospital and prayed for my mother. It was Sunday, Octo-ber 10, 1999. When I returned home the phone rang and my father and I picked it up

95

at the same time. "Mr. Le," the doctor said, "I don't think your wife is going to make it." I was speechless and stunned. Not one word came out of my mouth.

My father, my 10-year-old brother and I went straight to the hospital. While driving, I looked up into the clear night sky and said, "You wouldn't do this to me." Nobody really told me if there was a God or not, but for weird reasons, I knew somehow there was a creator or God. Even with this knowledge, I still thought that God was way too big to ever notice me. My life was already miserable and if my mother, who was the only person on this whole entire planet who loved me, left me behind, I thought I would die.

Arriving at the hospital, I rushed up the stairs and turned the corner to her room. I saw the nurses, but they just glanced at me and looked away. To my horror my mother's body was covered with a white sheet. I screamed at the top of my lungs, pulled the sheet off and jumped on her body, crying, "You can't leave me, you can't leave me! I'm sorry, I'm sorry!" I started cursing at God, "What kind of God are You to take everything away from me?" Words came out of my mouth that should never be said to God.

I went to school the next day; I couldn't stay home. In Spanish class, a Christian girl gave me a Scripture from the Bible. I told her, "Thanks," but in my mind I just thought it was a piece of junk. Then she gave me a hug. Elizabeth was a pretty girl and very sweet. She was the type of person I would never hang with because she appeared so innocent. But something about her caught my attention, the same way the guy who prayed for my mother did. It wasn't their looks or appearance, but it was the joy and love inside of them. I was desperate for that type of joy and love, so I started hanging out with Elizabeth and going to Bible study with her. Things at home were really bad. My father and I were fighting, depression hit me big time, and I was dreaming about killing myself.

I don't know why I kept hanging out with Elizabeth since she was a Christian. She never preached at me; she just loved me. She and the guy from Bible study kept asking me to church, but I always made up some excuse. One day, I finally agreed to go. When

97

we walked into the church, I saw a lot of people raising their hands, dancing and singing. *This is church?* I thought. *What a bunch of weird people on crack!* Standing with everyone else during worship, I thought, *Why are these people crying and raising their hands?* As I began to read the lyrics of the song, I felt some sort of warm heat come over me. I fell down onto my knees and started crying. Then I heard the voice of God telling me, "Karen, I'm the One you are looking for. I'm the love that will satisfy you. I'm the One who has a plan and a future for you." I whispered back to God, "How can You say that after all I have done and said to You?" All I heard back was, "Karen, I love you." I cried, unconcerned that my makeup was running down my cheeks. From that point on, my life was never the same. Now after three and a half years, my relationship with my father is awesome! I love him and my brother. My life has gone from darkness to light. I will never be the same.

For Karen to get saved, she needed the dynamic anointing of a church service. If you aren't planted in a church, where will you bring your friends who need to experience the power of God, demonstrated in the corporate anointing, to get saved? Sure, you could take them to a Bible study, but there are dynamics that take place in the corporate gathering of a local church that you can't reproduce on your own. There is a reason why the author of Hebrews instructed the Christians to "consider one another in order to stir up love and good works, not forsaking the assembling of ourselves together, as is the manner of some, but exhorting one another, and so much the more as you see the Day approaching" (10:24-25). We need the local church!

99

A PLACE OF DISCIPLESHIP

We also need a place of discipleship where we can bring our friends. One of our high school men's cadres had an invite night. They planned a big basketball tournament and all the guys were supposed to invite their friends. Josh, one of the cadre's regular attendees, invited his friend Cody whom he had been praying for and witnessing to for about a year. Josh was shocked when Cody agreed to come.

After playing basketball, some of the guys began sharing their testimonies about what Jesus had done in their lives. Then the cadre leader asked if anyone wanted to start a personal relationship with Jesus Christ. Cody responded, got saved and was filled with the Holy Spirit. He has been discipled in his cadre ever since.

As much as individuals need the local church to help bring in a great catch of fish, churches need each other to effectively reach a city. Generation Church can't reach 130,000 young people alone; therefore, we need other churches. Where we are weak, other churches are strong.

100

THE MALL CONCEPT

I believe that the days when churches compete against each other for a few healthy fish are over. It's time we understand the mall concept. Retailers have discovered the power and profitability of being in a mall, which has greater customer appeal than a lone store. Why? Because of the variety of stores the mall can offer. The same principle is true with churches. We all offer Christ to people, but each church has its own unique strengths that meet different people's needs. Working together only makes us more effective. For example, our church doesn't offer professional Christian counseling, but a church a few miles down the road has an excellent counseling program that we regularly recommend. We are part-nering with them to share in the harvest. As a result, more people are getting helped and saved.

A PRAYERFUL PLACE

*Father, I thank You for the Body of Christ
and the men and women You've sent to work
in my life. Surround me with people whose strengths
balance out my weaknesses. I pray that You
would help me to submit to my pastors and
parents so that we can work together to see Your
purpose come to pass. Help me humble myself and
ask them for help and prayer.*

*Help me to be a friend who can work with
others to see people saved. Thank You for filling my
life with people who love You and want to see Your
kingdom come and Your will be done. Show me how
I can serve the ministries of others so that even more
people can come to know You.*

Note
1. Bible Explorer, *Strong's Concordance* (Austin, TX: Epiphany Software, 1999), CD-ROM, s.v. "partners."

101

11

THE CHALLENGE OF **COMPREHENDING** GOD'S LOVE FOR SINFUL PEOPLE

PERHAPS YOU'VE HEARD THE OLD TALE ABOUT THE AMERICAN SHOE SALESMAN WHO WAS SENT TO A REMOTE REGION OF AFRICA. Soon after he landed, he wired his manufacturer, "I want to come home. Nobody wears shoes in this part of Africa." So they brought him home and sent another salesman who sold order after order. He wrote the home office, "Everybody here needs shoes!"[1]

These two salesmen had different perspectives. A person's perspective can determine the type of result just as different perspectives brought different results for the two shoe salesmen. Perspective is a powerful principle in successfully reaching people.

EVERYBODY HERE NEEDS JESUS

If we, as people-reachers, do not possess the biblical perspective of God's love for sinful people, we will end up like the first shoe salesman as we try to escape a world filled with people who do not want God. We will see our neighborhoods, schools, communities and cities as God-forsaken places that will never "wear shoes." Therefore, we might as well go home.

The Church needs Christians who possess a perspective of faith that says, "Wow! Everybody here needs Jesus. I have a lot of work to do." People may not seem to want shoes. In fact, they may even say no to the shoes at first, but wait until we start wearing them around town. Our perspective must be like the second shoe salesman: "Everybody here needs shoes!"

If we don't comprehend God's love for sinful people, we'll end up being like that one kid in the neighborhood who owns the sports gear everyone plays with. Without fail, someone makes the guy mad and he takes all his stuff and goes home, leaving the rest with nothing. As Christians, we cannot get mad and go home with all the stuff, leaving the world behind with nothing.

It is time to see people the way God sees them. If you are a high school student, you ought to walk down your hallways and respond to all the compromise and perversion by saying, "Wow, everybody here needs Jesus. This is a great opportunity!" Pastors, you should walk the streets of your city confessing how blessed you are to live in a city where everybody needs Jesus. What an opportunity! That's how the second shoe salesman saw the needs of people, and so should you. Every sinner represents an incredible opportunity to share Christ. Every perverse person has potential to experience God. Every godless individual is one more soul you get to bring to Christ. It is this faith perspective that can change a city.

PETER SAW IT

Our perspective changes when we have a revelation of God's unconditional love. This is what happened to Peter in Luke 5:8:

> When Simon Peter saw it, he fell down at Jesus' knees, saying, "Depart from me, for I am a sinful man, O Lord!"

Imagine what Peter must have felt after Jesus used him as a participant in this incredible miracle. He must have felt incredibly small. He knew that good things happened to good people, and he knew he was not good. Overwhelmed with condemnation, he decided to put a stop to this horrible hypocrisy. He asked Jesus to leave. Why? Because he knew that his lifestyle didn't warrant such a great miracle and financial blessing. He was a recipient of the gospel, the good news of mercy and grace.

The love that Jesus pours out on our behalf is not based on our lifestyle of good works. It is based on His unconditional love for all humanity. It is here that Peter began to comprehend God's immense love for people. Peter saw how much Jesus loved him, a sinner. Jesus used this opportunity to develop in Peter the right perspective and to shape him into the great people-reacher he was destined to be. The Scripture says, "Peter saw it." It was not just the great catch of fish he saw, but he also saw, most clearly, the outrageous love Christ has for sinners. Peter saw the extravagant, unearned love of God firsthand.

WE NEED A FRESH PERSPECTIVE

Let's look at a Scripture that reveals our need to understand the enormity of God's love:

> That Christ may dwell in your hearts through faith; that you, being rooted and grounded

in love, may be able to comprehend with all the saints what is the width and length and depth and height—to know the love of Christ which passes knowledge; that you may be filled with all the fullness of God (Ephesians 3:17-19).

Peter was just beginning to understand the extent of God's love when he "saw it" (Luke 5:8). In order to see the extent of God's love, we must see the cavern of our own sin. So it was with Peter. That day out on the boat, he had the realization of his own worthlessness, which enabled him to clearly see God's overwhelming worthiness.

107

This understanding was essential for Peter's preparation to "fish" for sinful people. We, too, must have a revelation of God's love for sinful people, which is best experienced in a personal relationship with Him. If we try to reach the young people of this generation without a proper understanding of God's love for them, it will lead to a lifestyle absent of compassion and sinners will conclude that they don't deserve God's unconditional love. Yet neither do we deserve His outrageous love. God's love knows no boundaries; it is capable of cleansing the most despicable transgressions.

If you have a wrong perspective—only seeing the world through the stained-glass windows of your church and concluding it to be doomed to hell—the time has come for you to revisit the place where you received undeserved love.

A PRAYERFUL PLACE

Lord, I thank You for rescuing me from my cavern of sin. It was love that led You to the cross for my sin. I pray that same love would break my heart for people. I want to know the compassion and love that You feel toward them. Help me to see them through Your eyes, that I might be moved beyond my own capacity for love. God, let Your love fill my heart. Let me know the width and length and depth and height of Your love that surpasses all knowledge. Let me be filled with all of the fullness of You. Thank You, Lord.

Note
1. Paul Lee Tan, *Encyclopedia of 7,700 Illustrations* (Rockville, MD: Assurance Publishers, 1979).

12

THE CHALLENGE OF **COURAGE** IN THE FACE OF FEAR

ROSARIO MURAT OF VALENCIA, SPAIN, DREAMED OF OWNING A SAILBOAT HER ENTIRE LIFE. Once she was old enough to work, she saved her earnings for twelve years until she finally had enough money to purchase her dream. The big day came and her beautiful sailboat arrived. She promptly took the sailboat and had it permanently cemented in her backyard. Confused, many friends and neighbors asked why she would do such a thing. She simply explained, "I'm terrified of the water."[1]

Fear will make you do the dumbest things. Can you imagine saving for twelve years to buy a sailboat only to put it in your backyard and never use it for its intended purpose? Unfortunately, many of us do the same with the gospel. Instead of using the gospel to save sinners, we decide to keep it unexposed in the backyards of our Christian communities. Just as a sailboat is meant for water, so the gospel is meant for sinners. Once we comprehend God's love for sinful people, the only thing that could hold us back from sharing the gospel is fear.

LOOK FEAR IN THE FACE

Fear is perhaps the greatest enemy of every soul winner. To overcome fear, we must face it. Sometimes we think that by doing outrageous feats we will overcome our fears. Not so! Fear is only overcome and dealt with when we make a focused, daily decision to walk in courage.

Eleanor Roosevelt once said, "You gain strength, courage, and confidence by every experience in which you really stop to look fear in the face. You are able to say to yourself, 'I lived through this horror. I can take the next thing that comes along.' You must do the thing you think you cannot do."[2] We must face fear with faith every day.

One young lady in Generation Church named Bethany decided to take on this challenge. Here is what she experienced:

> I started high school with high hopes of taking my campus for Jesus. Having just graduated from an eighth-grade class of

thirty people, I only had three friends. Yet God spoke to me to have an evangelistic rally in the high school football stadium. While I believed God and even made new friends easily, I was still terrified by the thought of sharing my faith in front of my peer group.

I told God I would pray for my friends and invite them to church, but I couldn't share the gospel.

As the year went on, people began praying for me to have boldness whenever I went to the altar for any type of prayer. I tried to surround myself with bold friends so that I could just smile and go along for the ride, but I only was deceiving myself, as I pretended to do the work of an evangelist.

At a Generation Church conference that year, Pastor Judah preached a message on overcoming fear.

I began to weep as I thought of the people at school who didn't know God. I ran to the altar call, begging God to set me free from the fear of witnessing to people.

I believed God had set me free, that His perfect love had cast out the fear that had been holding me back (see 1 John 4:18).

111

That week I approached one of the other members of my high school Bible study, knowing that if I didn't speak to him now, I probably never would. "I think God wants me to speak at the rally," I said, terrified of the words that came out of my mouth. He told me to go for it, so I began to prepare.

I'll never forget the way I felt standing before 500 classmates and faculty. That day I wasn't thinking about my insecurity. I prayed, and I knew that God would speak through me if I stepped out to obey Him. I approached the platform and shared my story of how Jesus pursued me when no one else wanted to be my friend. He kept me close to Him when my parents got divorced.

I had never felt such a confident presence of God as when I took that microphone. That day about thirty of my friends accepted Jesus Christ as their Savior. I realized the joy of laying down what was comfortable for me in exchange for the love of people. There's nothing like seeing your friends come to know God. It's well worth it.

112

CATCH EVERY MAN, WOMAN AND CHILD

In Luke 5, Jesus commands His disciples not to be afraid. He says, "Do not be afraid. From now on you will catch men" (verse 10). Jesus makes it very clear that we are not to allow fear to hold us back.

Here Jesus gives us two steps to overcoming fear. But before we investigate this, we need to understand where the fishermen are coming from. Peter and the boys are dealing with great fear despite the fact that Jesus has just given them this incredible, undeserved gift. The potential profit from this great catch is overwhelming all by itself. I am sure they wonder how they will ever repay Jesus. In their eyes, this gift requires them to live and perform at a certain level of which they are incapable.

The disciples are full of fear because they are still full of themselves. Fear originates in self-centeredness. They think that the only way to live up to this great gift is to work harder and be better. Yet Jesus wants the disciples and us to discard this fear-filled thinking.

He tells the disciples, "From now on." In other words, forget how you used to think. Everything changes for the disciples from that moment on.

113

They learn to think right and do things God's way. Similarly, we need to renew our minds and allow God to eliminate our fears.

Then Jesus says, "You will catch men." Jesus assures His disciples that just as they catch fish, they will also catch people. All they do that miraculous day is respond to Jesus' commands. He adjusts their focus, bringing the disciples to a point of total reliance on Him. This is where true courage begins. This is what Bethany experienced as she obeyed God and preached at her high school rally.

I recently came across this brief synopsis of a radical missionary, David Brainerd, which illustrates how we can live courageously when we rely wholly on God:

> While David Brainerd, one of the most celebrated of our missionaries, was laboring among the poor Indians on the banks of the Delaware, he once said, "I care not where I live, or what hardships I go through, so that I can but gain souls to Christ. While I am asleep, I dream of these things; as soon as I awake, the first thing I think of is this great work. All my desire is the conversion of sinners, and all my hope is in God."[3]

Courage is found when we loose ourselves in Christ. Just as David Brainerd was courageous enough to give his entire life to a people in need, we can live courageous lives when we lean completely on Christ.

Doing things God's way means we bear His name and His reputation. He takes over and we trust in His grace. Have you ever had a big, physically strong friend at school? Just being with that person gave you boldness. It didn't matter who was nearby, because as long as your friend was with you, you were safe. When we begin to trust in God, it doesn't matter who is around us or how tough the circumstance. We will boldly share Christ.

115

Jesus wanted His disciples to understand that He would empower them to catch people in the same way that He empowered them to catch fish; therefore, they had nothing to fear. We must allow this truth to take root in our hearts, too. We have nothing to fear. If we simply obey Him, trusting that He has a supernatural catch waiting for us, we will never turn back in fear.

PUSH BEYOND YOUR FEARS

"Courage is fear that has said its prayers."[4] True courage—the ability to push beyond our fears—is

THE **CHALLENGE** OF . . .

found only in God. The degree to which we find ourselves trusting and relying on God is the same degree
to which we will possess courage. As long as we continue to depend on ourselves, fear remains a factor.
Yet when we find our courage in God, we will move
beyond superficial, momentary action to a lifestyle
in which fear does not determine our choices.

Let's close with Eleanor Roosevelt's statement:
"You must do the thing you think you cannot do."
I can't think of a better definition to define courage.
Simply put, courage is a characteristic that pushes
us beyond our fears. It is this rare and powerful
quality that allows a seemingly small, frail and timid
individual to rewrite history.

A PRAYERFUL PLACE

Lord, I thank You that Your perfect love casts out all
fear and that Your love compels me to do what I
would normally be afraid to do. I pray that You
would rid me of my selfishness and help me to make
courageous decisions to reach out to people. You have
not given me a spirit of fear but of power, love and a
sound mind (see 2 Timothy 1:7).

God, I pray that as I courageously activate my
faith and step out, there would be a demonstration of

*Your Spirit's power. I ask that You would cause
me to love people despite the fear of rejection. I put
my confidence in You and pray that You will give me
the mind of Christ and great boldness in every
opportunity. I believe in You and Your ability to
move me beyond what I want to do in order to do
what You have destined me to do.*

117

Notes

1. Paul Lee Tan, *Encyclopedia of 7,700 Illustrations* (Rockville, MD: Assurance
   Publishers, 1979).
2. John C. Maxwell, *The 21 Indispensable Qualities of a Leader* (Nashville, TN:
   Thomas Nelson Publishers, 1999), p. 42.
3. Tan, *Encyclopedia of 7,700 Illustrations*.
4. Maxwell, *The 21 Indispensable Qualities of a Leader*, p. 37.

13

THE CHALLENGE OF **COMMITMENT** IN THE AGE OF COMPROMISE

Before peter and the other disciples had the miraculous encounter with jesus, they only followed him part-time. They listened to His teaching and participated in His miracles, but they didn't quite have everything they needed to answer Jesus' call to catch people. They weren't wholly committed to the cause of Christ.

True commitment isn't just a matter of listening to, teaching or reading a book and agreeing with it. Commitment isn't just trying something for a little while to see if it works. It is not being inspired by a good story to do something and then stopping as soon as the emotion wears off.

In the following story, William Stewart demonstrates true commitment:

Thomas S. Stewart injured one of his eyes with a knife. A specialist decided that it should be removed to save the other. When the operation was over and Thomas recovered from the anesthetic, he discovered that the operator had blundered the surgery by removing the sound eye, making him totally blind.

Despite the tragedy, he decided to pursue his law studies at McGill University in Montreal, Canada. Thomas was able to do this with the help of his brother, William Stewart, who read to him and accompanied him through all the different phases of college life.

Thomas, the blind brother, came out at the head of his class, while William came second. William practically made himself a seeing medium for his blind brother.[1]

The true commitment that both William Stewart and Peter demonstrate for us involves forsaking and following. Too often we try to follow Christ before we forsake everything. Imagine if Peter had tried following Jesus with his boats, nets and entire catch of fish behind him. He wouldn't have been very effective.

LEAVING SOME STUFF BEHIND

Picture this: A young man has heard the message of reaching people and is following Christ's example of compassion. He is waiting for an opportunity to hand somebody a card inviting him or her to church, and he finally spots the perfect person. He steps out in courage. But wait! He has a basketball in one hand, his girlfriend's hand in the other, a shopping bag on one shoulder, a messenger bag on the other shoulder, a backpack on his back, a fanny pack around his waist, cargo pants filled with CDs, and a cell phone clipped to his belt. How is he going to hand over the card? But this young man is determined. He walks over to the person without regard to all his stuff and kindly asks, "Excuse me? Would you like to come to church? Our church is awesome. If you come, your life will be free from all kinds of stuff. You can be free like me! Just reach into my back pocket and grab a card." If someone invited you to church in that manner, would you go?

121

Even though we may not always look that distracted on the outside, it could be a picture of what is happening on the inside. Somehow we try to follow Christ without first forsaking things that He asks of us. "Forsake" means "to renounce or turn away from entirely."[2] It is time for us to leave some things behind.

Not only do we need to forsake sinful things in order to commit ourselves completely to the cause of Christ, but at times we also need to forsake good things. Peter actually had to leave behind the miraculous catch of fish that Jesus gave him. Scholars tell us that Peter caught anywhere from three to twelve months' wages in that one catch. That's a lot of money! Yet he left it all behind to follow Christ and fish for people. Would you be willing to give up $30,000 to follow Christ?

FOLLOWING JESUS' REPRESENTATIVES

The second part of genuine commitment is following. Luke 5:11 says that the disciples "forsook all and followed Him." What does it look like to follow Christ? Following simply means to walk behind the person in front of you. This seems easy, except that Jesus Christ isn't physically walking in front of you on a daily basis. So how do you follow Him? It's actually pretty simple: You follow Jesus' representatives whom He has put on earth. Perhaps it is your parents, pastors, teachers, civil authorities, or others in your life. You follow Jesus by obeying your authorities, the Bible and the voice of the Holy Spirit.

COMMITTING TO THE CAUSE OF CHRIST

Jesus said in Matthew 16:24, "If anyone desires to come after Me, let him deny himself, and take up his cross, and follow Me." Our desires for Christ will lead us to deny our flesh. Our commitment must run this deep. Jesus clearly states that if we have a longing to come after Him, we must be willing to commit everything to Him.

Our commitment to Christ must dictate every area of our life: what we want, what we think about most, what we use our money for, what we do with our leisure time, the company we enjoy, whom and what we admire, and even what we laugh at.[3] As we read this list, we need to ask ourselves if all of these areas reflect our commitment to Christ.

123

Here is a story of one young man who effectively reached his mother for Christ:

> When I was 15 years old, I rededicated my life to Christ. God radically touched me and changed me. My mom and I lived in a two-bedroom apartment just north of Seattle, Washington, in a suburb called Mountlake Terrace. Both of my sisters had already moved out of the house. They were both living on their own before even graduating from high school. It was just my mom and me.
>
> I can't say that things were always easy or that my mom and I saw eye to eye on

everything. In fact, we didn't really see eye to eye on anything. This was primarily because I had decided to follow Jesus and my mom had not. She had spent earlier years in the church, but due to some mishaps by both her and the church, she wasn't too into it. So when I started going to church, youth group and other church events, it made things even harder between us.

Whenever church stuff or anything that concerned God came up, she was always very negative and would yell or cuss. This was hard on me. I felt alone. I wanted to leave home like both of my sisters. However, one thing kept me at home: I wanted my mom to get right with the Lord, and I wanted to be the one to help her do it. When everything in me wanted to leave, I stayed.

It was not easy at all. I had to give up all my selfish attitudes and any rebellion in my heart. I was forced to cling to God. Tear-filled prayers of anguish for my mom were not out of the ordinary. There was nothing else to do; there was nowhere else to go. I wanted my mom to live for God.

Judah Smith

After completing high school, I stayed in the Seattle area to attend school at Northwest Bible College. I regularly saw my mom on certain nights for dinner or a movie or to drop by and say hey. I took her out on date nights and brought her flowers. I wanted to show her the love of God and not just tell her about it. At certain opportune moments, I said little bits about God or told her something that I was studying at school. She liked helping me with my studies, but she was still very much turned off to church. Yet I kept at it.

Through this process, I continued to invite my mom to church, but she always refused. One night she saw my church on TV. She said that she happened to be up and saw it, and she liked it. What? My mom saw my church and liked it! This was a mighty move of God. The same person who hated church was now somewhat positive about it. For me this was a miracle, but the greatest one was in the making.

My mom finally attended a service at City Church's Easter service in 2002. That Sunday she raised her hand for prayer. That

Sunday she responded to the altar call in front of thousands of people. That Sunday she rededicated her life to God. That Sunday I saw my prayers answered.

On the way back to the car, my mom mentioned that her rededication to God was some time in the making. I really wasn't too surprised by this, because for five years, I had prayed for, fasted for and loved my mom to God. Now, after five years, I saw the fruit of my commitment.

What we need today is a resurgence of true commitment. We have enough compromise and self-centered individuals seeking their own desire. The times demand a new kind of leader, a new breed of young people who carry a cause bigger than thinking about themselves. If we are going to usher in God's grand purpose in an age of compromise, then we must raise the standard and commit ourselves wholly to Christ.

I believe we can reach the world in our generation. I trust that the stories, Scriptures and statements within this book have inspired you to new levels of faith and hope for the people you live with and walk by every day. As you put God's Word into practice, you will see the great harvest you long for. As you lay down this book, my prayer is that you would find great joy and fruit from sharing God's good news with people everywhere.

A PRAYERFUL PLACE

Father, if there is any baggage in my life that keeps me from my commitment to You, I pray that You would reveal it to me right now. I give You my desires, my energy, my motivation, and my abilities. I thank You that You are a faithful God and that You give me the power to keep my commitments.

I pray that even in the midst of a compromising generation, I would shine as a holy, consistent reflection of Your commitment to me. I pray that as people see my dedication to loving You and loving them, they will know that You are the God they want to know.

127

Notes

1. Paul Lee Tan, *Encyclopedia of 7,700 Illustrations* (Rockville, MD: Assurance Publishers, 1979).
2. *Merriam-Webster's Collegiate Dictionary*, 11th ed., s.v. "forsake."
3. Harry Verloegh, *The Quotable Tozer I* (Camp Hill, PA: Christian Publications, 1984), p. 165.